START SAYING

YES

Improving Customer Experience and Sales
Through Positive Messaging

MATTHEW ROUSE

Cover designed by Matthew Rouse
Editing by Kari Rouse
Back Cover Photo by Craig Brubaker

Matthew Rouse
Visit my website at hookseo.com

Printed in the United States of America

First Printing: December 2018

ISBN-9781790351602

CONTENTS

For Faith & Kari

The largest enemy of change and leadership isn't a 'no,' it's a 'not yet.' 'Not yet' is the safest, easiest way to forestall change.

—SETH GODIN

START SAYING YES

Servers in Oregon Always Say No

I saw Anthony Bourdain speak before he passed away. He's not a big fan of Vegetarians and Vegans, to say the least.

I surmise that he took it a bit easier on them than usual since I saw him in Portland, Oregon.

If you want to get your hybrid-electric rental car run out of Stumptown quickly, get on a stage and make fun of Vegans and Vegetarians... or cyclists.

People can be touchy about these subjects in Portland.

But let me quote him from *GoodReads* which is similar enough to what he said to make my point.

The point however, has nothing to do with being a Vegetarian, and everything to do with saying, "No."

> *"Vegetarians are the enemy of everything good and decent in the human spirit, an affront to all I stand for, the pure enjoyment of food. The body, these waterheads imagine, is a temple that should not be polluted by animal protein. It's healthier, they insist, though every vegetarian waiter I've worked with is brought down by any rumor of a cold.*
>
> *Oh, I'll accommodate them, I'll rummage around for something to feed them, for a 'vegetarian plate', if called on to do so. Fourteen dollars for a few slices of grilled eggplant and zucchini suits my food cost fine."* —Anthony Bourdain

The point he is trying to make is different than mine, but the result is the same. It's cheaper and easier to give a vegetarian a plate of grilled vegetables, than to prepare a meal containing a well-cooked animal protein.

Remember, we're in Portland, Oregon here. The Portland Metro Area has a chain of vegan cupcake shops and gluten free bakeries. If there is anything people here have, it's food choices.

With a vegetarian population sometimes clocked as high as 10% in parts of the United States, your establishment should be ready.

* * *

Scott, my business partner at Hook SEO Digital Marketing, came into town for a visit a while back. A group of us went out for dinner at a local Italian Restaurant.

We got on the topic of poor technical support and I think everyone knows how bad technical support has gotten in the past decade.

After hearing about everyone's poor experiences, the topic soon shifted to general state of poor customer service that seems to be everywhere.

"Have you ever noticed that servers will tell you 'No' for anything in Oregon?"

Scott continued, "That doesn't normally happen in most other places. But go to any bar or restaurant in Oregon and you will hear them tell people 'No' over and over."

I thought about this briefly and realized I had heard the word, "No" a lot lately. Maybe it was just because Scott brought it up, but now I am remembering all the No's I've heard recently.

It's like when someone tells you to look at how small Ceelo Green's hands are. And now you can't see anything but his tiny hands every time you see him. Good thing his popularity has been waning since its height back in 2014.

Nothing against Mr. Green, but look it up on the Internet. I think it's a mental thing. Once you notice it, you can't un-see it, like the Internet rumors of Megan Fox's "toe thumbs."

Our drinks come and it's time to order. My wife eats mostly vegetarian and today is one of those times.

"Could I get the chicken pasta, but without the chicken, maybe just with some vegetables instead?"

Wait for it...

Guess what the answer was?

"No, but we can do the 'no chicken' part though," the waiter says after forcing himself not to roll his eyes.

You can tell he doesn't care... at all.

"They can't just throw in some vegetables instead of the chicken? I'll pay for the chicken, I just want vegetables instead, if that's not a problem." Kari was quite polite about it.

"Well, what kind of vegetables?"

That was a good question. Well, for starters, how the hell does my wife know what vegetables they have? She doesn't work in their kitchen.

Secondly, why don't you ask the kitchen staff, or a manager or just own the problem and figure it out yourself?

The reason is that he doesn't give a shit about us... the "guests" who are the whole reason he has a job in the first place.

Anthony Bourdain would *have loved* to cook my wife a plate of vegetables for 10% of the cost of a chicken breast. As he put it in his live show, "any chef would be saying Cha-Ching!"

Kari, my wife, continues with a confused look on her face.

"I don't know, like some onions and peppers and mushrooms maybe? Can they just throw a handful of vegetables in it? I don't know what you have."

"Well, we don't normally do that, but I guess I can ask them." He then just walks away, having not taken the rest of our tables orders or saying something polite such as, "excuse me for a moment."

In the end, Kari ends up with pasta and a couple pieces of onion and a mushroom in it. This is considered one of the few "nicer" restaurants in the area.

We haven't been there since.

I don't want you to think I am bashing on servers here. I know many fabulous servers who give great service, but they are often the exception these days, not the rule.

In Todd Duncan's book, *The $6000 Egg,* he shared a similar story about a restaurant in Newport Beach where they refused to cook a fried egg to put on a burger.

It was at a restaurant they frequented and the ensuing arguments from staff and management as well as repeated attempts to contact the owners were all met with confrontation and more terrible service.

They were trained to say 'No' from the top down. The owners treated the managers confrontationally. The managers were now confrontational with the staff, which taught the staff to be confrontational with the customers.

Todd estimated that the loss in revenue to the restaurant by him not bringing his family, friends, and clients there was at least $6000. And that was just the first year... and before he wrote a best-selling book on the subject.

You are only as good as your last customer interaction.

One incident does not a restaurant make, but the point is this.

In both sales and service, people are so quick to tell customers "NO," for even the simplest of requests, that people are used to it.

Like the staff in this example; was our Italian Restaurant server trained to say No?

Probably.

Not directly, but he probably asked for a substitution on a meal previously and was told "no," by the manager, or he was hassled by the kitchen staff for the request.

Maybe he just hates vegetarians?

I don't care what the reasoning is.

If you take nothing else away from this book, this is what you need to ask yourself.

Do you want your guests or customers to be treated this way?

Do You Know What Your Salespeople Are Telling Your Customers?

My wife Kari and I set out on a mission.

We like to live a bit of a minimalist lifestyle and it was finally time to break down and buy a new BBQ.

A nice BBQ, with several burners, a thermometer in the lid and maybe even a side burner.

We spent years with crappy old used BBQs, and it was high time we spent our hard-earned money on a new one!

We had just bought our first home and a huge dining room table for entertaining, so the BBQ was going to round out our entertaining accoutrement.

We live just down the road from a couple of those "big box" hardware stores. They have literally hundreds of BBQs, so it seemed like a good place to start.

We looked them over for quite some time and narrowed our search down to two different Weber® Grills that we liked.

I flagged down the young lady working there and asked if she was the BBQ "salesperson."

Soon, you'll discover why I put "salesperson" in quotation marks.

Kari wanted to know what the difference was between two BBQ models. Both had the same number of burners and similar features, but one was $20 more.

"We want to buy this one, but this other one looks the same. Why is it $20 more? We can't find any difference between them."

The sales associate answered the question (it was some accessory it came with) and then proceeded to tell us, "You don't want to buy a BBQ now though!"

Our interest was piqued now!

Was a big sale coming up? Was a new model being introduced? Did she know of a better model at the same price?

"All the BBQs are going to go on sale in a couple months. Actually, I even think some of them are on sale at Walmart right now."

Hint: We were not at a Walmart. (We haven't been to a Walmart in a long, long time; but that's a story for another book.)

We came in to this store specifically to purchase a BBQ.

We already planned out how to get it home and put it together. We were going to make some burgers and roasted vegetables (remember the vegetarian part) and we had quite the day planned for our shiny new BBQ.

Kari and I talked about it some more but all our confidence in this purchase was gone. Now we were questioning our decision to buy one right now.

The "salesperson" had let the wind out of our sails. If we bought it now, we would be losing money. Some undisclosed amount of money, and basically it was now a bad decision to buy it.

We were going to pay "full price" for the BBQ, on the spot. We were ready to make the purchase, and a positive, up–beat salesperson would have closed the deal in 30 seconds.

What should have happened:

"YES! This one comes with a rotisserie attachment. That's great for cooking poultry or a nice big roast."

I would get excited about that too. I want to BBQ a roast! This is why we want a BBQ. Tell me more, energetic and positive salesperson...

"You're going to need some bigger BBQ tools. And make sure you get a cover to keep it looking new for years to come! With our delivery service, we can deliver it today, put it together for you and have you cooking in less than 3 hours! Want me to wrap this up for you?"

YES.

Wrap that up, give me the BBQ tools, the cover, an extra tank of propone and throw in some Tiki torches!

We're going to be cooking dinner on our first new BBQ in years tonight. I can already imagine our friends faces light up as they see me taking that roast off the grill, with my apron on and a smug look on my face...

That's not what happened though.

Our "salesperson" decided she would tell us No.

I'm sure she thought she was being helpful, but by saying 'No,' she was just raining on our parade.

The store lost the revenue, a high margin sale, and selling all those high profit accessories too.

Do you think that Kari and I want to tell all our friends the story of how we had the wind taken out of our sails and decided not to buy a BBQ?

Instead of a happy customer, they made me feel like I was making a poor decision. Maybe I was.

That's not up to them.

People are telling themselves a story about cooking on the grill surrounded by friends and family enjoying themselves, the children running and playing, the smell of their steaks on the grill and the sun shining down.

Like it or not, a BBQ is an emotional luxury. It's not just an outdoor stove.

Maybe a better salesperson could have signed me up for a store card, or rewards program to generate loyalty and future sales.

Saying YES makes you more money.

Saying YES gets people excited about purchasing the things they want.

Saying YES gives you the chance to make positive changes in the lives of others.

We ended up getting a Traeger Grill a couple years later from Kari's Dad, who found it at an auction.

We love it. Kari especially loves it. She cooked for some friends and family and had great results and now every dinner party or holiday, she's cooking something on the Traeger.

She is telling herself a story about the great food, the fun times, and the compliments she gets on her cooking.

Train yourself and your staff to help people tell themselves a story about positive changes in their lives.

And make sure you know what your employees are telling customers.

If it was your business, would you want your staff telling people to buy your products on sale somewhere else?

START SAYING YES

Owning the Problem

Another day, another restaurant, another all too common customer service issue.

Ironically, it was the same day I started writing this book, the morning before we went there for lunch.

It was a few parents and our collective tribe of small children.

One of their offerings is "bottomless fries" that come with your meal. One of the guests asked our server if they could get some fries for the small children while we waited for our meals that already come with "bottomless fries."

Help keep the toddlers happy and it will cut down on the noise and reduce the chance of annoying other guests nearby. It's a win-win.

NO.

"Well, I mean, Yes, but we would charge you for it, but No, not for free. Not until after we give you your meal. Then it's bottomless fries."

No. Well, sort of Yes, maybe, but Yes costs more.

Thanks, we'll pass. That's absurd.

He should have started with YES.

"YES, I could get you some fries for everyone to share right now, it would just cost a couple bucks extra, if that's OK with you."

YES, we would have paid for them.

But I am also a bit confused.

Do the potatoes cost more before we ordered than after we ordered?

This is just splitting hairs with no actual basis in cost and realistically, what does a handful of fries for a toddler cost compared to the happiness of your guests and the other guests around them?

How much do you value a positive customer experience?

I'm not one to complain in stores or restaurants, and I don't leave nasty reviews. I even wrote what is currently the top-rated Google result for <u>getting rid of fake reviews</u>.

I just make mental notes and decide to return or not return. A lot of other people do this also.

It's called "Dark Social" when people talk about things online and you can't see those things.

Like it or not, the conversations are happening. You and your company are just not a part of it.

Want to see your sales drop? All it takes is a few people in a local market to say, "You guys won't believe what happened to me today at _insert business name here_." And then share it with a hundred of their friends online.

If you think you need to fear negative reviews, you need to fear dark social more. It's what kills your business without you knowing about it.

What you should take away from these examples is how these employees presented a negative attitude toward your customers.

Training employees, sales staff, or your customers that 'No' is the rule, and not the exception, results in a poor customer experience This will ultimately will drive those customers to another establishment.

It will increase negative reviews, drive hidden negative conversations on dark social and word of mouth as well as creating an environment that isn't fun to work in.

Unhappy managers, with unhappy staff, serving unhappy people.

They are business killers.

When your competitors say YES, they gain the favor of your customers, spread positive word of mouth, and enjoy repeat business.

START SAYING YES

Negativity Posted on the Door

NO FOOD
NO DRINKS
NO PETS
NO CHECKS
NO PHOTOS

This sign hangs in the entry way of a small store in Newport, Oregon, in a trendy little beach front area on the coast of the Pacific Ocean.

There are little boutiques and coffee shops and little rental houses, and a couple art galleries. It's beautiful, you should visit there.

I can understand wanting to protect your merchandise from food and drink, or no pets in a food store, but no photos?

There is a better way to approach these types of issues.

"Please cover drinks with lids and we welcome food in containers. We want to ensure your purchases are stain free!"

"We love pets too, and licensed service animals are welcome. Oregon State Law prohibits non-licensed service animals. We apologize for any inconvenience."

People understand that you must follow the law to stay in business. If you have a good rationale for a "rule" then it is acceptable.

Now think about the no-photos part.

Everyone has a camera/video camera in their pocket that walks into your store.

Every one of them can snap a photo, tag themselves as "checked in" at your store, and share those photos with hundreds of people.

If anything, you should be encouraging photos.

Set up an area specifically made to take photos. How many people can walk past one of those big paintings with the faces cut out and not take a photo?

Now let's get back to my coffee, because if you know me, I love coffee.

The chance of someone spilling a coffee with a lid is slim in a little boutique. Yes, I'm sure it happens rarely.

Imagine how many customers are walking around with their coffee in the morning while on vacation. Strolling down the street with that vacation money burning a hole in their pocket. They would have bought that little scarf or handmade jewelry piece at your boutique, but alas, the first thing they read was "NO DRINKS."

A while back, I walked into a shop by accident that said, "NO DRINKS" on the door and my wife reminded me, pointing at the sign.

The lady at the counter waved her hand at me and said, "Oh it's OK, we don't mean coffee."

Do you remember that movie, The Princess Bride, with the character named Vizzini who keeps saying, "Inconceivable!?"

"You Keep Using That Word, I Do Not Think It Means What You Think It Means"

NO DRINKS to anyone outside your store does not mean, *"NO DRINKS, BUT COFFEE IS COOL, BRING THAT COFFEE ON IN HERE."*

It means *don't come in my shop if you are holding a beverage*.

I watched people with safely closed bottles of water who were looking at the door, shrugging and moving on. People with their coffee protected by lids, look in the windows and then walk into the shop next door instead.

Why are these stores so eager to turn away potential customers before they even make it through the front door?

Everywhere we went.

NO PHOTOS.
NO DRINKS.

Do you know who has enough money to buy your highest priced products?

People who have enough money to go on vacation and drink fancy coffee.

People who have the latest cell phone, with an amazing camera and a good data plan.

That's who.

Do you have signs signaling to potential customers that they are not welcome?

Being Available

No one explained the chain reaction of progress sparked by the word YES better than Eric Schmidt, Google's executive chairman, during his commencement address at the University of California at Berkeley:

"Find a way to say yes to things. Say yes to invitations to a new country. Say yes to meeting new friends. Say yes to learning a new language, picking up a new sport.

YES is how you get your first job, and your next job.

YES is how you find your spouse, and even your kids.

Even if it's a bit edgy, a bit out of your comfort zone, saying yes means you will do something new, meet someone new and make a difference in your life, and likely in others' lives as well. ...

YES, is a tiny word that can do big things. Say it often."

YES can be hard to do.

YES takes a lot of effort, especially in these days where 'No' is everywhere you look.

The Millennial Generation has grown up with 'No' built into their environment by design.

These days, 'No' isn't just an old store owner with a "No Skateboarding" sign, shaking his broom at some kids on his sidewalk like when I was a kid.

Cities install metal "pig ears" also known as "skatestoppers" which are metal bumps on railing and curbs so that if skate boarding kids use them, they will fall down.

Park benches are made with strange curves and arms rests in the middle of them now to stop people from laying down on them.

Corners of office buildings have metal bumps on the concrete to stop the homeless from sleeping there.

Many cities employ fake cameras or even cardboard cutouts of police cars on bridges to try to stop people from certain behaviors.

Whether you agree with these things or not, they are all 'No' by design. Our young adults have grown up being told not to do things at every corner, while at the same time being told that they need to be positive thinkers.

We all need to try to see past the negative environments and create positive change.

Saying YES can change your outlook on the world and change your life.

If you *work hard and smart*, and start saying YES, you can probably do things you never thought you could.

A good example is how I never considered, even a few years ago, that I would be writing a book about positive business messaging. Let alone writing my third book.

Saying YES can take you to new places you never thought possible. Places you never knew existed.

By being positive, you are opening the doors of possibility. You are allowing yourself access to new opportunities, new projects, new people and new journeys.

There is also a lot of value in knowing when to say No and I will get to that soon, but positive risk taking can change your life.

Build YES into your environment and things will start to change around you.

It's all about saying YES to the difficult things that move your business forward.

Delegating a task you know you can do better than someone else is hard. Really hard. For example delegating sales calls.

Of course, your salespeople can't sell as well as you. They aren't you.

You're the captain of the ship, so you've probably been selling longer, and in many cases, you built this company from the ground up, so no new salesperson is going to sell as well as you can.

If you're a graphic designer or a copywriter or a painter, or a plumber, or a wedding planner... hiring someone to help do your job means hiring someone who isn't going to be as good at it as you are.

Saying YES to them, gives you time to build the business. Saying YES means giving up one thing so that you can have more time to say YES to more important things.

Say NO to a $10/hour task so that you can say YES to a $200/hour task.

Say YES to scheduling an hour of time every week where you do nothing but work on your business.

No Phone. No Email. No Interruptions.

When we are always playing schedule Tetris, we don't give ourselves time to work on problems that can move our organizations forward.

It could be as simple as the first hour I set aside to work on my own business a few years ago. In that time, I started our newsletter back up and committed to weekly emails to our favorite clients and friends.

It was tough at first to make the time in the schedule and stick to it.

But after a while it was habit. For example, very Wednesday for me is email newsletter day.

I said YES to doing something that moves my business forward.

Since then, we've attracted several of our biggest and happiest clients from the small enrollment in our weekly marketing emails.

I said YES to delegating one of my tasks, which allowed me to say YES to the newsletter.

This generated hundreds of times the revenue compared to the cost of delegating the task in the first place.

It took more time and training up front, and it was difficult to let go of the reins a bit, but in the long run, the benefit was greater revenue, and a time savings that allowed me even more time to work on the business.

They love that I bring helpful, timely information to them without spamming them with another sales email or short-term play for revenue.

Most companies collect email subscribers and social media followers and then they spam them to death every time they need to hit a sales target, or they are a little short on revenue.

You must respect your potential customers and treat them like your good friends. Talk to them. Respond to them.

Say YES to them.

Saying YES is like a snowball.

It takes some time to get it started, but once you get it rolling down the hill, the opportunities you create will keep increasing in value.

START SAYING YES

Why Say Yes?

A few years ago, I watched a presentation about the Fermi Paradox by CEO, Rand Fishkin.

He was comparing the lack of "exceptional marketing" with the paradox of why we haven't found alien life in the universe.

Mathematically, there should be aliens everywhere. It should be like Star Trek, where we search for intelligent life, and every place we look, someone already lives there.

This is the Fermi Paradox.

The theory is that there is some "great filter" that almost no species or civilization can overcome to accomplish interstellar travel.

Because of the inability for alien life or civilizations to get past this "filter" holding them back from travelling the universe, we're essentially alone in our corner of the Milky Way.

In the lives of people, saying Yes is the Great Filter.

Now let me explain.

Saying Yes helps you generate serendipity.

ser·en·dip·i·ty (noun)
– *the occurrence and development of events by chance in a happy or beneficial way.*
"a fortunate stroke of serendipity"

Now before all the realists start rolling their eyes thinking this is about *manifesting* or some new age thinking, it's not.

But if you are a manifestation believer, here's your proof that it works... just not the way your yogi says it works.

* * *

4 years ago, I had never been to a business networking event, a local Chamber of Commerce, or anything like that.

I needed to get my business moving in the right direction as we were making a little revenue, but things were tight. We were bootstrapping a marketing agency from nothing.

We had a few web design clients and some payment processing clients my business partner, Scott still had from a previous business.

I was getting more into podcasts and after a little searching, I found one about business and they suggested visiting a networking meeting with my local chamber.

Was it hard to go to an event that I knew nothing about in a room full of people I didn't know?

YES.

If you don't say YES to difficult things, you don't get anywhere in life.

I met a couple people at the first event I attended, and they suggested I come back and visit again, which I did.

Fast forward a couple years and I was doing lunchtime workshops for small business owners at the Hillsboro Chamber's *Build-Your-Business* events.

I joined several networking groups, each time entering a room full of people I didn't know.

I started saying YES to every presentation or workshop or speaking event I could. (Thank you again for the advice, Rand Fishkin.)

I said YES to crowd funding my first book after watching an interview between Ryan Hanley and Guy Vincent on a now defunct video interview platform called *Blab*.

On the interview, Guy said "You can reach out to me" and gave his email address and I said YES and sent him an email with my first book idea.

Soon after that, I had a skype chat talking about my book idea, and less than a year later, my first book was published.

It went on to sell hundreds of softcover copies and we gave away a couple thousand digital versions. We weren't getting rich selling books, but that's not what they were for. I'll get back to this in a couple pages...

Here was a string of opportunities where I said YES. That opportunity lead to a new one, with another difficult decision I had to say YES to.

This is how I learned the most valuable lesson of all when it comes to saying YES and taking chances.

People who say YES stand out. They are different.

Writing a book showed me what I could accomplish with a little hard work, dedication, and goal-setting.

Being a public speaker gets a little easier, a bit less nerve-wracking and a little more fun every time I do it.

Saying YES transformed my life and my business.

Let me get back to the first book my company published, **Crush SEO: Learn How to Market Your Local Business Online**.

While my local competitors were handing out business cards, I was teaching workshops, giving presentations, and handing out signed copies of the book.

As my favorite author and speaker, Seth Godin says, "In a crowded marketplace, fitting in is a failure. In a busy marketplace, not standing out is the same as being invisible."

START SAYING YES

Be a YES in a World of NO

There is effectively infinite choice in the modern business world. Just like there is infinite shelf space on Amazon, there are thousands of results for every Google Search.

The average person only visits about 1 in every 1 Million available websites in their lifetime.

For example, there were about 5000 books a month published in the early 1990's but that number is over 50,000 per month now.

The invention of Amazon has provided endless isles with essentially infinite products and books to choose from.

When your only choice was a book store, you could only buy the books they put on the shelves. Now you can get any book.

These days, anyone can publish a book. You don't need an agent, a publisher, a cover artist... you just write it and upload it to Amazon.

Some people have estimated as many as half the books on Amazon have never sold more than 5 copies, ever.

Now let me ask you this.

Why did you buy this book?

Did it stand out because of the cover?

Did it show up when searching for another book?

It is more likely that you are reading this book because someone told you about it.

The first rule (and third rule) of *Fight Club* is you don't talk about *Fight Club*.

In this movie centered around Tyler Durdan and his "underground boxing clubs" the clubs keep growing and people end up starting their own Fight Clubs in other cities.

If they aren't supposed to talk about it, why are there so many Fight Clubs opening up?

The reason is the same reason for why a book club grows or why one great food cart has a huge line up every day instead of another.

It's why an "indie" video game made by one programmer in his spare time turns into Minecraft.

It's why some churches expand without advertising and it's why Dropbox is now virtually a household name.

People feel good when they can recommend something they love to a friend.

The recommendation factor is multiplied when people have the same world view, that is, they have the same beliefs about the thing they are sharing as the people they are sharing it with.

If you want people to talk about you, you must have something about you that is different. You need a unique thing about yourself, your product, your service, or your business.

Think about *Little Miss Matched*. They sell colorful non-matching socks for young girls. And they sell them in sets of three.

The girls can wear any combination they want, and if you lose one, not a big deal. When they are on the schoolyard, what do you think they are showing their friends?

Being different drives word of mouth.

My hope is that this book will help you make positive changes in your business and your life.

If you have someone you would like to share it with, I hope that you will.

START SAYING YES

There's a Few Things You Need to Say No To

Saying YES can be difficult. It should be difficult sometimes if you're doing it right. It's difficult to show up every day and give it our all. It takes dedication.

Your brain should be telling you to run away.

Your brain wants you to do less and conserve energy. To not take a chance at embarrassment or standing out and bringing attention to yourself.

Thousands of years ago, when standing out meant that you could be ostracized from your clan or tribe to fend for yourself in the wild, it could be deadly.

Embarrassment is when we feel there is a disconnect between how we are being seen and how we feel we should act or respond in public.

The same holds true here. We've been trained over hundreds or even thousands of generations that we need to try to fit in. To be part of the tribe.

Now that human beings have "won" the food chain war, standing out is an advantage instead of a danger. Fitting in is now a failure.

There are over 2000 ads shown on the Internet for every single human being on the planet. Every single day.

Signal to noise ratio is the amount of useful information available versus the proportion of the entirety of information.

Basically, how much is good – signal, versus how much is noise that you don't care about.

On the Internet, the signal to noise ratio is astonishing.

You want to be the signal, not the noise.

Saying YES isn't enough. You must also clean up the "noise" in your own life and your own business. You are going to have to be able to say No.

You will need to audit your time and see what is valuable to you or to your organization.

The first thing you need to do is understand that you want to say YES to that speech, proposal, leading the team, or volunteering for that event.

You need to say NO to people using your time and energy for their personal benefit, without consideration for your goals.

Sure, spending time with your toddler isn't going to make you more profitable, but it doesn't mean it's not valuable time. Be selective.

Everyone has heard of the 80/20 principle and it applies to your business productivity and your positivity.

Most often 20% of your clients produce 80% of your revenue. Also, nearly 80% of your hard work only yields about 20% of your results.

There are also 20% of people in your life who are wasting 80% of the time you spend on them. Stop letting them steal your time.

Most people have also heard that you are the sum of the people you spend the most time with. Start saying NO to people you don't want to become and spend time with people you admire.

I don't mean walking up to them and saying, "No, Jim, I'm not hanging around with you anymore. You're just not the caliber of people I want to become!"

Do it as tactfully as you can, because you don't want to invite confrontation. If you must, you may need to break it to some people that you don't have time for them.

"Joan, you've been a great client all these years, but I need to level with you. I have seven employees now all pressing for a little bit of my time and I don't handle this type of work in the company anymore. I am going to ask that you contact Charlotte in support about your widget problems from now on because she is able to give you the support you deserve."

Delegate.

Your sales guy won't be able to sell as well as you can.

The designer you hired doesn't have your style.

That new coder is going to write slower and have a hard time debugging your previous version because, darn it, he just doesn't know the software like you know it.

That support person doesn't know the customers like you do. They don't care like you do.

Of course, they don't!

It's not their company. They didn't build it from the ground up, and they aren't the boss.

But if you're going to reclaim some of your time to do bigger and better things, you're going to need to trim the fat somewhere because you can't play schedule Tetris any longer.

Say NO to that late-night TV show that is stealing your sleep.

Say NO to the fast food and YES to a few more vegetables.

Every time you say NO to something, you are opening some room to say YES to something else.

You're saying YES to something better.

Instead of running those reports that Bob in Accounting can run and analyze, go work at that Charity event.

Sure, it's going to take Bob twice as long to do analyze that report as you would, but he'll figure it out eventually.

Business Author Rory Vaden often talks about the *30x Rule*. If you can train someone to do a task for you, even if it takes 30 times longer to train them as it does to do the task yourself, it'll pay off in the long run.

Think about it for a second. If you need to run a report that Bob in Accounting can do for you once a week, it'll pay off soon.

If it takes you 10 minutes to run the report and analyze it, but it takes you 300 minutes to train Bob, that seems like a lot of time. That is an hour a week for 5 weeks. But after that it's done.

Now you save 10 minutes every week. In one year, you will gain back 520 minutes of your time and Bob will be glad that you trust him enough to let him handle this task. You gained 220 minutes, or 3 hours and 40 minutes of your life back in the first year alone.

Best part is, it probably won't take Bob that long to figure it out. Bob's a smart guy, that's why you hired him.

And what happens if you don't get him to do your reports and you can't go to that charity event you were invited to?

You're not going to meet that nice lady who runs a startup that could use the services of a company just like yours.

And poor Bob is stuck doing his regular job.

You didn't say YES to the difficult thing and stayed doing the thing you've always done.

By not saying YES, you've thrown away the opportunity to make a connection with someone or discover a new hidden opportunity.

Saying YES means being available for luck to find you.

Because luck doesn't find you at your desk.

You cannot generate serendipity when you aren't reaching out and stepping up and doing uncomfortable things.

Say NO to the ordinary but say YES to the hard work of putting yourself out there.

"Out there" is where the good stuff is.

Say Yes to Marketing

Robert Cialdini has turned the marketing world around with something called Pre-suasion. This practice focuses on a simple fact of human nature.

What you say or do before you deliver your message to a potential customer can leverage your success.

There's a story that a man in France was trying to chat with women and get their phone numbers so that he could call them later to go out with him on a date.

He was walking around in a shopping center trying different locations to see if it would help improve his chances.

His success rate averaged 13% no matter where he was, except for one place. When he was in front of a flower shop, his success rate doubled to over a quarter of the women he asked out.

The backdrop of flowers signaled the potential for romance in the brains of the ladies he was asking, and his success rate doubled.

People who plan out what they will say and do before they deliver a marketing or sales message are the people who excel. They are not just persuading people, but pre-suading them by helping them get into a positive frame of mind.

So how do you put people into a frame of mind that is conducive to the message you want to deliver to them without being deceptive or trying to "trick" people?

The answer is saying YES.

And there are a lot of ways to say YES.

Today I went for lunch with my Project Manager, Jeremy, to a little family run Mexican Restaurant... with loud country music playing in it. But alas, that odd fact is for another book.

We asked for more chips, YES.

More salsa? YES.

I ordered a burrito with guacamole...

Stop right there!

You know what happens when you ask for Guacamole? The server will say, "Guacamole is $2 extra. Is that OK?"

This happens so much that people around here wear t-shirts that say, "I know guacamole is extra."

I bet there are about 1 in 20 people who ordered guacamole, didn't notice it was clearly marked on the menu as $2 extra, and then complained about the cost.

Just give it to them for free. You know why? Because giving 5% of people a couple dollars' worth of guacamole to keep them happy isn't going to crush your bottom line.

Arguing with people who ate it and don't want to pay for it and then having them tell all their friends that your restaurant sucks, will kill your bottom line way faster than writing off a few avocados.

"I apologize Ma'am. Is it OK if I just take that off your bill?"

YES, that's OK.

Think about what you would do if you owned the little shop I mentioned previously that is next to the cute, busy, hip coffee shop in that vacation town on the coast.

What would your sign say?

COFFEE DRINKERS WELCOME!

YES! You're our people. Come see what we have made for people just like you!

Remember the BBQ salesperson?

"It sure is a beautiful day out for a BBQ, isn't it? (YES) Can I help you folks get set up with everything you need to make the most of your new BBQ? (YES)"

It's not just about my dream of going to a restaurant where my wife, Kari, can get a few vegetables instead of chicken in her meal without an argument.

It's about using positive messaging to change your business and your life.

At this point, I think we can both agree that a little positive messaging and saying YES can take your business a long way.

Now let's talk about how to use positive messaging to build your business through the power of referrals and customer experience.

Saying Yes to More Referrals

Referrals are the true bread and butter of almost any business. The cost to acquire a referral is virtually nothing and they are generally your best clients.

People who have been referred stay with your business longer, spend more, complain less, and they are 50% more likely to refer someone else.

The problem with most businesses is that their referral strategy is what I call, "pray for referrals."

If you're in the church business prayer might be a good strategy but when it comes to referrals, you're just putting your organization at risk.

Often organizations who see a big "boom and bust" cycle that has no rhyme or reason to it, are usually living off random referrals.

When they get a few referrals, they get busy and when those referrals stop, the business drops off with the management scratching their heads why it's suddenly gotten so slow.

What you need is to train your customers to start saying YES to telling their friends about your business.

Jay Baer wrote a book in 2018 called *Talk Triggers*. In 2018 Seth Godin wrote *This is Marketing*. The common thread in these two books by the champions of modern marketing is how knowledge about a business spreads.

The one thing people remember about your business needs to be built into the process of how you follow up with people.

We will come back to this in a minute, but first I want to ask you a simple question.

Why doesn't everyone who's able-bodied do some pushups and sit-ups every morning when they wake up?

We all know that they are good for us.

Nothing is stopping us from doing them.

So why don't we do it?

The answer is that it's easier to sell aspirin than vitamins.

It's hard to say YES to the sit-ups because that future healthy person is someone else. We don't see our future selves as the same person as we are now. There is a disconnect.

If we take vitamins every day we might be able to avoid that future headache, but we don't know that now.

If we have a headache now, we'll buy aspirin. We'll even buy some just to have laying around because it's great to have it when we need it.

People avoid discomfort.

People will attempt to avoid future discomfort if they have felt it before.

Another thing we need to agree on is that people remember the exceptional.

When you were a "caveman" thousands of years ago and you went from bush to bush eating little red strawberries the tried a black one that was rotten, it was an exceptional experience.

Exceptionally bad, but it stood out. You never ate another black strawberry again as long as you lived.

People are hard-wired to remember the exceptional.

Your brain is designed to filter out the ordinary.

It takes calories and effort to consider things. Every time you must think about something it could take your attention away from something that could kill you. A predator, or an environmental factor.

We remember the positive exceptions also.

When we found that the best berries grew in a certain spot. We didn't remember where all the berry bushes were, but we remembered where the BEST berry bushes were.

Now let's get back to what Jay Baer calls *Talk Triggers*.

They are memorable moments when someone engages with our business, and are exceptional compared to our competition.

It needs to be the creation of a moment that is *remarkable*. Remarkable as in something someone will make a remark about to someone else.

It also needs to be relevant to your business or the relationship you have with your client.

Therefore, unless you're Starbucks, sending Starbucks cards as gifts isn't really a memorable moment.

If you knew they loved Starbucks, and you sent them a Starbucks mug, with a gift card in it, or maybe some coffee they can make at home, now you're headed in the right direction.

This remarkable moment you are creating must be affordable so that it can be done repeatedly. You cannot give away a free car with every purchase of a plumbing repair. You're not Oprah.

Finally, it needs to be *operational.* It must be a part of your process in dealing with your customers.

The easiest way to accomplish this is to start with your follow up process. You should have a process and document that process.

Write it down. Then follow it and have your staff follow it.

Everyone gets contacted after you've completed their service and gets reminded of how awesome and different you really are.

Because now is the time they will tell their friends about you. Now is the time they are most likely to refer you.

Say YES to creating a memorable reminder to your clients and not just contacting them again when you want money.

I want you to start saying YES to following up with your clients and turning it into a remarkable moment that they will tell their friends about.

Committing to this follow-up is a not just a step in the right direction, for most people it is the first big step in changing their business forever.

The Big Step

Let's talk about how you can create a follow-up process that will change your business. It's not difficult, but it does take some planning and creativity.

Most businesses have a sales process that looks something like this:

1. Customer becomes aware of your business through research, advertising, referral, etc.

2. Customer looks you up online.

3. Customer contacts your business and engages with a salesperson/dispatcher/front desk staff person.

4. Once the customer has started the process of purchasing or scheduling, they are handed off to accounting for payment or invoicing.

5. No one ever speaks to them again unless there is a problem, they haven't paid their bill, or you want to sell them something else.

It's time to create a follow-up process that is so remarkable that you will get more referrals.

How you follow up and when you follow up will be different for each business but it's something that will make you stand out from your competitors.

It can be as simple as a hand-written note.

When you finish doing work with a customer you can write them a card, or use an online service like Send Out Cards. (I recommend <u>Lori Bitter</u> if you need help with Send Out Cards.)

It's important that a person who knows the customer or served the customer is the person who writes the note.

It needs to be short and relevant, and not a postcard. Because people throw junk mail postcards from companies in the garbage, but they put greeting cards on their desk or shelf.

It shouldn't have your logo on it. If your customer likes cats, send them a card with a cat on it. If your customer likes hiking, give them a card with some scenery on it.

It needs to be personal also. My old insurance agent sold his business a while ago. At some point, they spelled my name incorrectly and got my birthday entered incorrectly into their automated follow-up system.

Now every year, about three weeks before my birthday, I get a card from an agent I have never met with my name spelled incorrectly. Every year it reminds me that they don't care.

They are literally paying money to tell me how much they don't care. It's absurd.

Just say NO to the inauthentic, the afterthought, the thing that says, "I am pretending that I care."

Modern people have had every scam, sham, and automated marketing ploy beat them down for years. They see through the obvious automations and know it's nothing but garbage and noise.

Say YES to sending authentic, honest messages to your customers.

Say YES to contacting them when you aren't asking them for anything.

Make follow-up a part of your customer's experience, not just when you need money.

I met with my friend Johnny who works with an HVAC company just a few weeks ago. We talked about how they can improve their customer experience to compete in a competitive market.

"Let's say someone's furnace is broken, and it is very cold outside. The furnace needs a part that has to be ordered, so you can't fix it for a few days."

"What if all your trucks had a few spare space heaters in them? You drop off the heaters to tide them over until the part arrives."

"Maybe when you fix an air conditioner, you leave a little card on the counter that reads *This house certified comfortable by* _____. With your company's name and the name of the repair person on it?"

"Follow up with a card from the repair person. She can have a stack of cards and stamps in her truck and write the card at the end of the service call and drop them all in the mailbox when she gets back to the office."

Whatever system you put in place, you must understand the expectations of your customers and then exceed them for their benefit, not your benefit.

There is a local real estate agent that sends a house cleaner for a family who they helped purchase a home. They send the cleaner after the family moves in, so the cleaners can clean up all the move-in related mess and help the tired family take a break.

Though not directly follow-up related, The Magic Castle Hotel has a red phone by their outdoor pool. When you pick it up, someone answers with "Popsicle Hotline" and gives you some choices of which popsicles they have.

Then a staff person dressed in black and wearing gloves carries an entire tray of popsicles out to the guests, pool-side, free of charge.

Everyone who stays there, talks about the Popsicle Hotline.

My father is a professor of corporate strategy and travels a lot for work. One time he was staying at a Hilton Hotel and called the desk to ask if they had slippers since he had forgotten his and he likes to wear slippers at night in the room instead of his regular shoes.

Ever since that one call to the front desk, every time he stays at a Hilton Hotel, they have a pair of men's slippers in his room for him.

He doesn't have to call ahead or ask. They are just waiting there in his room, anywhere in the world he travels at every Hilton Hotel.

Exceptional ways to follow up with, or accommodate your customer's needs, are the vitamins your organization needs to take to grow your future business.

Having a steady stream of referrals and a sales pipeline full of potential customers takes the stress off you and your sales team.

Exceptional experiences don't have to be just done during your follow-up. You should endeavor to improve the experience your customer has at every interaction with your business.

Make a list of every touch-point with your customer and say to yourself, "How can I improve this part of the experience for my customer? What do *they* want?"

One thing my own company implemented is a process that takes an extra 10 minutes per customer and they love it.

We build websites for small to medium sized businesses and often the people are not very technically savvy.

When we finish their website, we don't just send them a login and password. We shoot a quick screen-recording video of how they get to the login screen for their new website. We show them how to enter their login credentials, and then how they can make basic changes to the website themselves without a developer.

We then email them a link to the video and they can watch it anytime they need to remember how to make a change.

Our customers love it and it saves us both time in the long run.

This is our talk trigger. Our remarkable moment during follow-up, also called an *operational differentiator.*

That's a mouthful, but it describes the way you can implement something into your business process that improves the customer experience, is repeatable, inexpensive, and will get your customers talking about the experience.

Once released in print, we plan to give two copies of this book to every one of our new customers.

One to read and one to share with a friend or colleague.

This is an operational differentiator that will make us stand out from competitors and give our customers a reason to talk about us.

How can your business make the extra effort that others are not willing to do?

How can you take the steps to not only say you have exceptional customer service, but to make it truly remarkable?

Say Yes to Incremental Positive Change

In his book, The One Thing: The Surprisingly Simple Truth Behind Extraordinary Results, Gary Kellar says this.

"Your next step is simple. You are the first domino."

Start Saying YES.

The small things that turn into habits, the processes you build into your business, are the small steps that bring in big results. They are the small hinges that swing big, heavy doors.

I've always been a self-starter, but a terrible finisher. I would start project after project and then move on to the next shiny object.

It's the part in the middle of a project, between starting and finishing that makes the difference between great success and mediocre results.

As Seth Godin calls it, *The Dip*.

It took me a long time to learn that it's the journey, not the destination where you create the most value. Getting past the dip.

The Dip is where you competitors quit or don't go the extra mile. Overcoming *The Dip* is where you start to make your business exceptional.

The journey is what improves you, your business, your character, you outcomes.

"Quit or be exceptional. Average is for losers." – *Seth Godin*

The fact is that average people have average lives and get average results because they avoid discomfort and settle for mediocrity.

They say NO to the difficult and uncomfortable things that set apart the people who make real change from the people who watch change happen.

They say YES to the couch and the television instead of saying YES to writing that novel or starting that business.

They put off doing the things that matter until those things no longer matter to them.

No one regrets all the times they tried hard to build a business or create a non-profit or shoot for the moon.

Everyone regrets the things they didn't do that they feel they should have done.

Start saying YES to those things now.

Being exceptional at what you do and how you treat people and how you serve your customers is never a bad thing.

Say NO to the things that waste your time or don't move you and your life and your happiness and your business forward.

Build YES into your life and your organization.

Everything you did before now is a "sunk cost."

It's already been paid for with time or money or sweat and hard work by the past you. It's a gift from yesterday you, to you now.

You can't get that time, money, or effort back so what you need to do is forget about all that and ask yourself, "what is my best path forward?"

From now on, you have the choice to say YES to that presentation, or that conference.

Saying YES is a key that opens doors to new opportunities. It's the new job you applied for or the promotion you are going to get by hiring a business coach while your counterparts are binge watching Netflix.

Saying YES means tearing down the "NO PHOTOS" sign on the wall of your gallery, and figuring out how to encourage your customers take even better photos.

Saying YES means re-writing the rules to agree with your customer instead of trying to force them to comply with rules. It's saying, "We love service dogs" instead of "NO PETS."

Improve your customer's interactions with your organization so that you can build a consistent referral stream and start saying YES to more success.

It's important to know when to say NO, to do it tactfully and with empathy but nothing good starts without first saying YES.

Make change happen.

Start Saying YES.

Prologue: Start Saying Yes Now

It's easy to read a book and feel great about the ideas in it and get that warm glow of accomplishment that comes with completing a task. But let's take it one step further.

I want you to walk away with this experience and prove to yourself that saying YES changes everything.

If you sell retail, you have a chance to mystery shop your own stores and see what your salespeople are saying.

If you do business over the phone, you can call your own office and see how your staff handle phone calls, or listen to your own voicemail message.

If you own a bar or restaurant, you can have someone ask the servers at your restaurant for a handful of vegetables instead of chicken breast.

Will they try to make the customer happy while making you more money, as suggested by Anthony Bordain?

If you're a real estate agent or a loan officer, are you keeping up relationships after you close a deal? Are you making remarkable, impactful follow-up or are you sending a bottle of wine as a closing gift and forgetting about them?

Do you follow up with your eCommerce customers after their purchases? Are you surveying them about their experience? Does your packaging and un-boxing experience match the value of the good you sell?

Is your customer service line there to build a stronger relationship with your customers or just a cost of doing business where you point out the fine print to get them off the phone as quickly as possible?

Does the customer who wants a pair of slippers need to call the desk every time they stay there?

When you change the relationship with your customers to be truly remarkable, you increase the value of yourself in your market.

You go from being A choice, to THE choice.

What is going to be your Popsicle Hotline?

It's your turn.

Start Saying YES.

Made in United States
North Haven, CT
03 July 2023

38516397R00067